# On the value and importance of an International Peace Trail

## A Project in Global Planning

**By Düg Fresh**

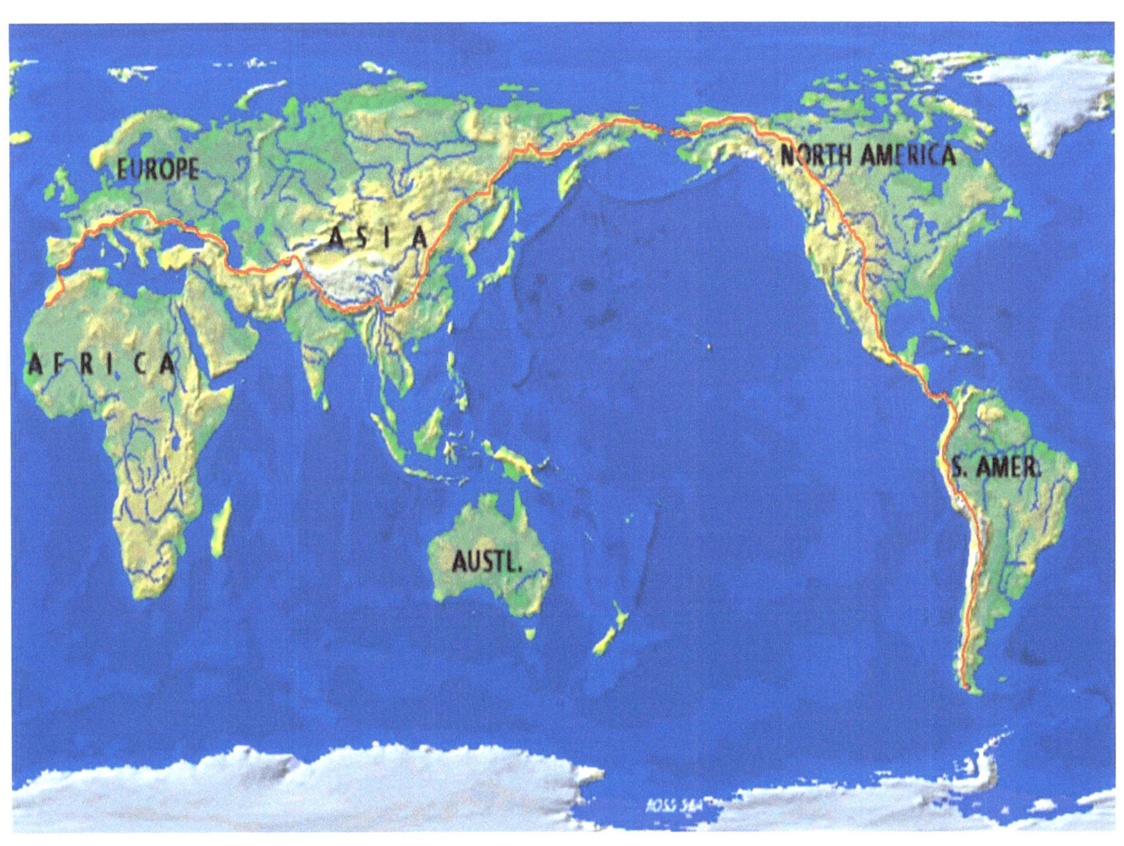



*"A footpath for those seeking fellowship with Earth."*

Proposed route for the *International Peace Trail*,
see appendix A for a brief description.

"The world is not given by his fathers, but borrowed from his children"

Wendell Berry
*The Unforeseen Wilderness: An Essay on Kentucky's Red River Gorge*, 01971[1]


"We have not inherited this earth from our parents to do with it what we will. We have borrowed it from our children…"

Moses Henry Cass
Speech in Paris for a meeting of the
*Organization for Economic Co-operation and Development*, 01974

# On the value and importance of an International Peace Trail

Note: the following is an excerpt from
*A Thousand and One Appalachian Tales, part non-zero*

Humanity's present rate of total energy consumption amounts to only one four-millionth of one percent of the rate of its energy income.

R. Buckminster Fuller
*Critical Path*, 01981

Long ago in my youth, I discover R. Buckminster Fuller's hefty tome *Critical Path*[2]. The book is full of near limitless optimism and reads in a manner seemingly intent on weaving a Gordian knot into every sentence!

Like some mad cosmic accountant, Fuller tallies Earth's expenses and finds enormous difference between what everyone *can* have and what everyone *does* have. He shows how everyone can live a life of abundant wealth and prosperity – how this dividend is available to us all - if only we can learn to cooperate, work together and stop perpetuating a system of haves and have-nots[3].

If only we can see what to Fuller seems so clearly apparent, a vast and wonderful future awaits us! What makes mankind so strange is that this should all be incredibly obvious: we have so much more to gain by working together[4] and everything to lose by not. And yet we persist in the not.

Needless to say, Fuller's book[5] is profoundly affecting. The future of Man-in-Universe no longer looks so daunting and impossible. It looks uncertain, improbable and even unlikely, but not impossible. There is a non-zero chance. After all, everything up until now has been equally improbable, *yet here we are*. Life is all about defying the odds[6].

Fuller has faith in the power and beauty of science, in the ability of the intelligent mind to rise to any challenge. He gives us a bold vision to follow, a *Critical Path* that can lead mankind to an ambitious and exciting new world, a world where there is sustainable peace and prosperity for all.

But with the horrific death of a close friend my life becomes a strange desperate search for this path[7], this doorway in the now leading to such a grand *Fullerian* future. Yet I cannot help but feel, in spite of all the hope and logic behind Bucky's writings, that we are long past such a critical path, long past the point of no-return. But though this may be so, we must never give up. We must ever find a way[8].

And, more than a decade later, a way finds me[9]! One day in 01997 an idea begins to take shape, a bold solution to the many problems facing mankind today: *The International Peace Trail*. In that beautiful idea, it becomes clear how a "footpath for those seeking fellowship with Earth," if built, can help lead to the very future I can only hope to imagine reading Fuller.

Back in 01984, practicing a form of creative visualization, I follow unfolding possibilities, bifurcations of the ever-branching present, to a future where Earth is once more transformed into a magnificent blue-green gem, resplendent in natural diversity and beauty. Poverty, hunger, disease and war are a thing of the past and everyone enjoys a standard of living many times what the richest have today. We have become an interplanetary species, a type 1 civilization.

But while this vision shows me a way, the sequence of events passes too quickly. I only remember it all begins with a vision quest and this begins in the Military. So, I muster up my courage and enlist.

The Air Force takes me to Europe and I cannot help but feel this somehow confirms I am heading in the right direction. There are many little synchronicities that no doubt holds only personal significance[10], but one event of incredible power, that I mention in *A Thousand and One Appalachian Tales: A journey along the A.T. and through the heart of Chapel Perilous*, is the profound experience at the Anne Frank House in Amsterdam. There are no words to express the ton of bricks that drops onto the core of my being from this encounter.

Next, in late 01987, when receiving an offer for an early release while almost simultaneously learning of the Appalachian Trail for the first time, I cannot help but feel that this too is another pile of bricks dropping at exactly the right moment to lead to the next step along the way.

After Katahdin, I return home to a small welcome of sorts. My friends christen me Fresh, *Düg Fresh*, and for a while life is good. But there lingers something restless deep inside. For many years I wonder, what now? I wander through various jobs: a canvasser for the Environmental Planning Lobby, a residence counselor for developmentally disabled adults. Eventually I find myself working nights as a delivery driver for a wholesale florist[11]. Here I'm able to maximize the opportunity to sit and reflect. What's the point? Why are we here? What am I supposed to do? I'm not entirely sure these questions have answers, let alone if they're even meaningful questions! So instead, I ask: *what can I do to make a difference?*

Long ago I fathom a secret of life: be kind to others, help where you can and if able try to leave things better than you find them[12]. But the questions swell up inside. You can't take it with you but you can leave it behind. So, what am I leaving behind[13]? And what, if anything, can I do to leave behind a better place?

From this strange confluence occurs, in 01997, the slow germination of an idea. As a result, a small website is built and the *International Peace Trail Project* is born. The IPT Project proposes "the creation of a global infrastructure linking together much of Earth's highest terrain and wilderness areas into a massive World-Wide Parks and Trails System. The main corridor of this system will be *The International Peace Trail*[14]."

In the development of this website, it becomes increasingly clear that to build the International Peace Trail is to help solve the seven major problems facing the world today: war, hunger, lack of education (ignorance,) poverty, pollution, extinction and disease.

Only everyone working together can build such a Trail. But in so doing, far more than solutions to preserving wilderness areas and restoring habitats can be found. As important as solutions to these problems are, through the cooperation it will require to build the Trail and forge the global will necessary to care and maintain it, can be found the foundation to lasting world peace and sustainable solutions to all these problems and more!

For example, global climate changes have clear links to the destruction of biomass[15]. Biomass is the total mass of living matter within a given unit of environmental area. Believe it or not, biomass is a vital part of our rich cultural heritage. It acts as a whole, like a thermostat, to reduce greenhouse gases, absorb carbon and stabilize the climate into temperate zones supremely suitable to life. As we destroy it, we destroy life; as we destroy life, we destroy our home, our heritage and our future. Clearly everything must begin with conserving and restoring biomass. The *Nature Conservancy* and the *Sierra Club* are excellent examples of organizations working in this area. Please support these groups and others like them[16].

Another example is top-soil. Pedogenesis is the process of soil formation and there is a serious crisis today – the topsoil is disappearing! Soil is a living thing. It requires organic matter to form. But use of chemical pesticides kills these organic components reducing living soil to lifeless dirt and dust. As good soil is lost, plants cannot grow[17] and more biomass is lost.

Thus, organic farming provides direct alternatives to the destruction of biomass through the use of natural methods that preserve and ensure a healthy environment for living soil, the necessary foundation for a healthy biomass and any sustainable system of agriculture[18].

With the restoration of biomass, climate will once again stabilize within a region ideally suited for capturing and distributing the life-sustaining, life-creating properties of the sun. As life flourishes mankind will once again gain reward through the incredible abundance of solar energy distribution in the rich flora and fauna of Earth. As this synergistically produces an increase in biomass, poverty and hunger will gradually diminish.

Also, as many diseases escape the confines of rain forests by excessive logging, a rich biomass will help to isolate and limit the spread of these diseases and reduce their geographical reach. For example, the Zika virus has its origins in the Zika Forest of Uganda and up until the 01950s is generally isolated to a narrow equatorial region. As temperatures rise, we will see an increase in otherwise rare parasitic infections such as *Angiostrongylus cantonensis*, or more commonly Rat Lungworm disease, mosquito-borne diseases such as Dengue Fever and chikungunya and frighteningly devastating fungal outbreaks such as Bd—*Batrachochytrium dendrobatidis*, which scientists attribute to wiping out almost 5% of all known amphibian species[19]!

The spread and ravaging effects of disease can also find further reduction by implementing a system of sanitation as proposed by the United Nations. More than 2 million people, mostly children, die every year from lack of sanitation and access to clean drinking water.

As those who involve themselves with these issues can tell you, solving the problem of disease is vital to solving the problem of poverty. So, by providing adequate drinking water and sanitation, the incidence of infant mortality due to disease and poor sanitation can drop as much as 75% according to a UN Study[20]. Again, only by conservation and restoration projects will this be possible.

For example, one of nature's greatest treasures is the aquifer. Aquifers are vital to providing fresh, clean water. Believe it or not, many aquifers are being encroached upon and destroyed by rampant development. The aquifer in the Albany Pine Bush, now a landfill for hazardous waste[21], provides distressing evidence in alarming detail. Furthermore, as these resources are lost, poverty will increase. It is only by preserving and restoring these areas, by protecting these resources, that we can reduce infant mortality rates due to poor sanitation and dirty drinking water. As infant mortality rates drop, poverty will further diminish, as will issues relative to poverty such as hunger and starvation, crime, war, and the untold suffering and consequences of war.

World peace comes from conservation of wetlands, preservation of aquifers, and the protection of natural habitats. Peace, like life, is synergistic. If you want to fight poverty, you must fight against the causes of poverty as well as its effects. Destroying wetlands impoverishes us all. Rolling over Aquifers in the name of urban sprawl only increases global poverty and disease. Strip mining, mountaintop removal, fracking and slash and burn logging not only increase everyone's risk of disease, these practices limit access to clean water and fresh air and accelerate global climate change[22]. Furthermore, none of these practices are sustainable. You will eventually run out of wetlands to pave, mountaintops to remove and deposits to frack. But the lasting damage will be done long before then, so long as non-invasive and sustainable methods are not implemented and employed.

Thus, protecting Earth's diminishing wilderness areas and natural habitats will go a long way toward helping to restore the rich biomass that will stabilize the environment and prevent or at least mitigate climate change and its consequence, climate wars. In all this the International Peace Trail can help!

The International Peace Trail Project envisions a World-Wide Parks and Trails System which will preserve, protect, restore and reclaim these natural resources and wilderness areas. Such a self-regulating system will work to preserve the diversity of plant and animal life from further encroachment and extinction, as well as limit the spread of disease, while protecting and empowering indigenous tribes, keeping them from poverty and providing a habitat for many endangered species.

By working to solve issues relating to disease and hunger, while providing education and sustainable growth, poverty will diminish whereby further peace will grow and the whole effect will become synergistically self-perpetuating and self-sustaining[23]. It's simple. The creation of the International Peace Trail will help create the world peace that will help create the International Peace Trail[24]. And this in turn will help create world peace!

It seems clear that any solution to the problems of war must first address the problems of poverty, hunger and disease. But before we can address these problems, we must first address the problems of Earth's dwindling natural resources. It all builds upon each other and at the foundation is the extremely rare and precious blue-green marble on which we all live. It simply will not do to address any one of these issues without first addressing the others.

Thus, behold the International Peace Trail: it will stretch around the world protecting and linking together wilderness areas, natural habitats, parks and wildlife areas. Where possible, the Peace Trail will follow and link together existing trails.[25] It will raise awareness and engender support and sponsorship, and more importantly, stewardship. It will provide a path for many sacred journeys and vision quests. It will inspire stories and tales that will unify a people. It will bring peace.

So, through a free hosting company the International Peace Trail website went up practically overnight. The purpose of the website is to promote the IPT Project and its primary goal: the creation of the International Peace Trail Alliance. The IPT Alliance will work together with local, state and world governments, the UN, Peace Corp and civil engineers to create the International Peace Trail, which in turn will help link, create, restore and sustain natural habitats and ecosystems globally through an interconnected worldwide parks and trails system.

This system will preserve and protect these lands and resources, restore biomass and bio-diversity, which in turn will reduce global climate change, pollution and the extinction of untold species of plant and animal life. By protecting and restoring these resources, global prosperity will grow. This prosperity will in turn reduce poverty and with it the problems associated with poverty: hunger and disease. And, as we eradicate the problems of hunger and disease, so too is do we eradicate poverty!

With the decline of poverty comes the further prosperity of the planet, which in turn will perpetuate the sustainable growth of these habitats and wilderness areas, which in turn will perpetuate further peace and prosperity, and so on. It is synergy in action!

With regards pollution, too much of anything is bad and too much $CO_2$ in our upper atmosphere is very bad. When there is robust biomass, $CO_2$ is easily captured by the life-enhancing life-affirming process of photosynthesis. So, two things must occur:

    1.) We need to cease releasing harmful gases into our air and harmful chemicals into our streams and rivers.
    2.) We need to capture and remove the tremendous amount of $CO_2$ and other pollutants we have already released.

*Because the effects we are experiencing now are from $CO_2$ released 20-years ago, we still have yet to experience the effects of all the $CO_2$ we have released since then*[26]! Please read that again. Because of years of obfuscation and disinformation stalling action, we have all but foretold our doom. But there are things we can do, such as tree-planting campaigns. Plants are our friends and we need them now more than ever. We need to stop taking Earth for granted.

There have been many campaigns in the last few years to plant more trees[27]. We need many more such efforts. There is a new estimate that planting 1.2 trillion new trees would absorb more carbon than current human emissions[28].

Certainly, we will also need to innovate other solutions through carbon-capture and solar technologies. But we also need to rebuild biomass from the ground up, starting with soil; this is the foundation of our sustainable future and the true wealth of Earth. It is with great wisdom that we name our planet after the life-giving soil upon which we live, for the true wealth of Earth is earth.

Another consequence of a warming planet is the loss of permafrost. Permafrost is a thick layer of soil in artic regions that remains frozen throughout the year. It is considered a carbon sink in that it removes carbon from the atmosphere. Approximately 24% of land in the Northern Hemisphere is, historically, permafrost and is trapping over the millennia massive amounts of carbon in the form of carbon dioxide and methane. However, the permafrost is currently melting and the release of these gases as a result has the additional effect of accelerating climate change and increasing the chances of a runaway greenhouse effect[29].

As the International Peace Trail envisions a series of trails linking parks, habitats and wilderness areas, it can help by spurring regrowth projects and by bringing attention to and expanding these wilderness areas, while helping to reclaim and restore other undeveloped lands around it. As such projects will work to rebuild biomass and capture carbon, the effect on permafrost will hopefully slow and reverse.

We need to create more parks, protect more areas and remove more pollutants and greenhouse gases from our global biome. Locally we need to plant more trees, use non-polluting renewable resources, use canvas totes and stop using plastic bags and other disposable non-reusable, non-biodegradable plastic items.

Globally, we need to support such initiatives to restore and rebuild the many diverse and wondrous habitats of nature: rivers and lakes, oceans and coasts, forests and soil, grasslands and prairies, deserts and arid lands, and arctic tundra, glaciers and high-altitude ecosystems.

The IPT can help focus these projects and expand on them. In so doing, temperatures will eventually return to optimal values for sustaining life. Furthermore, everyone working together to make this happen will engender world peace.

The goal of the International Peace Trail Project is, at first, to promote the idea of the IPT through its website. Then, as interest grows, it will hopefully inspire the global will to form both the International Peace Trail Foundation and the International Peace Trail Alliance. It will be through the efforts of this alliance that the International Peace Trail will be created and maintained. It will be through the efforts of the International Peace Trail Foundation that an IPT Fund will be created to sustain it.

With the creation of the IPT Alliance, a world-wide parks and trail system will be established, the main corridor of which will be the International Peace Trail. The IPTA will have chapters in every major city of the world. Each Chapter will provide maps and maintain a section of the Trail while providing Internetworking resources to independent groups and organizations dedicated to ecological, biological, geological, and sociological[30] issues. Chapters will become resources for conservation and restoration efforts, ecology and education.

The creation of the International Peace Trail is conceived of as occurring in three phases:

1. *Presentation*: Here a potential route [see Appendix A] and the ideas behind the IPT are put forward. Here the case is made that worldwide involvement can provide a sustainable framework for a lasting legacy of peace and prosperity for all.

   This book *On the value and importance of an International Peace Trail: A Project in Global Planning*, presents the case.

2. *Promotion*: The promotion of the IPT is continued with this book, with www.peacetrail.org and on social media.

   But to make the International Peace Trail a reality requires the efforts of a good many people to pick up where this work leaves off and create the *global will* that will lead to the creation of the International Peace Trail Alliance. Here we find a ring pass not. It requires you to overcome.

3. *Preservation*: This final phase will result in the completion and designation of the International Peace Trail as an official worldwide "footpath for those seeking fellowship with Earth," as well as providing a continuing blueprint for the development and expansion of a global parks and trails system.

   Chapters of the International Peace Trail Alliance will operate in every country of the world, manage local groups to maintain and care for the Trail, sell and distribute guides and maps, and participate in environmental education programs and restoration projects.

Preservation is envisioned to occur in four stages:

1. Creation of the International Peace Trail Foundation
2. Creation of the International Peace Trail Alliance
3. Creation of the International Peace Trail
4. Creation of a Worldwide Parks and Trails System

If you build it, peace will come. Have you been on the Peace Trail today?


If we recognize that every ecosystem can also be viewed as a food web, we can think of it as a circular, interlacing nexus of plant animal relationships (rather than a stratified pyramid with man at the apex)... Each species, be it a form of bacteria or deer, is knitted together in a network of interdependence, however indirect the links may be.

Murray Bookchin
*The Ecology of Freedom* (01982)


The Holy Land is everywhere.

Heȟáka Sápa (Black Elk)

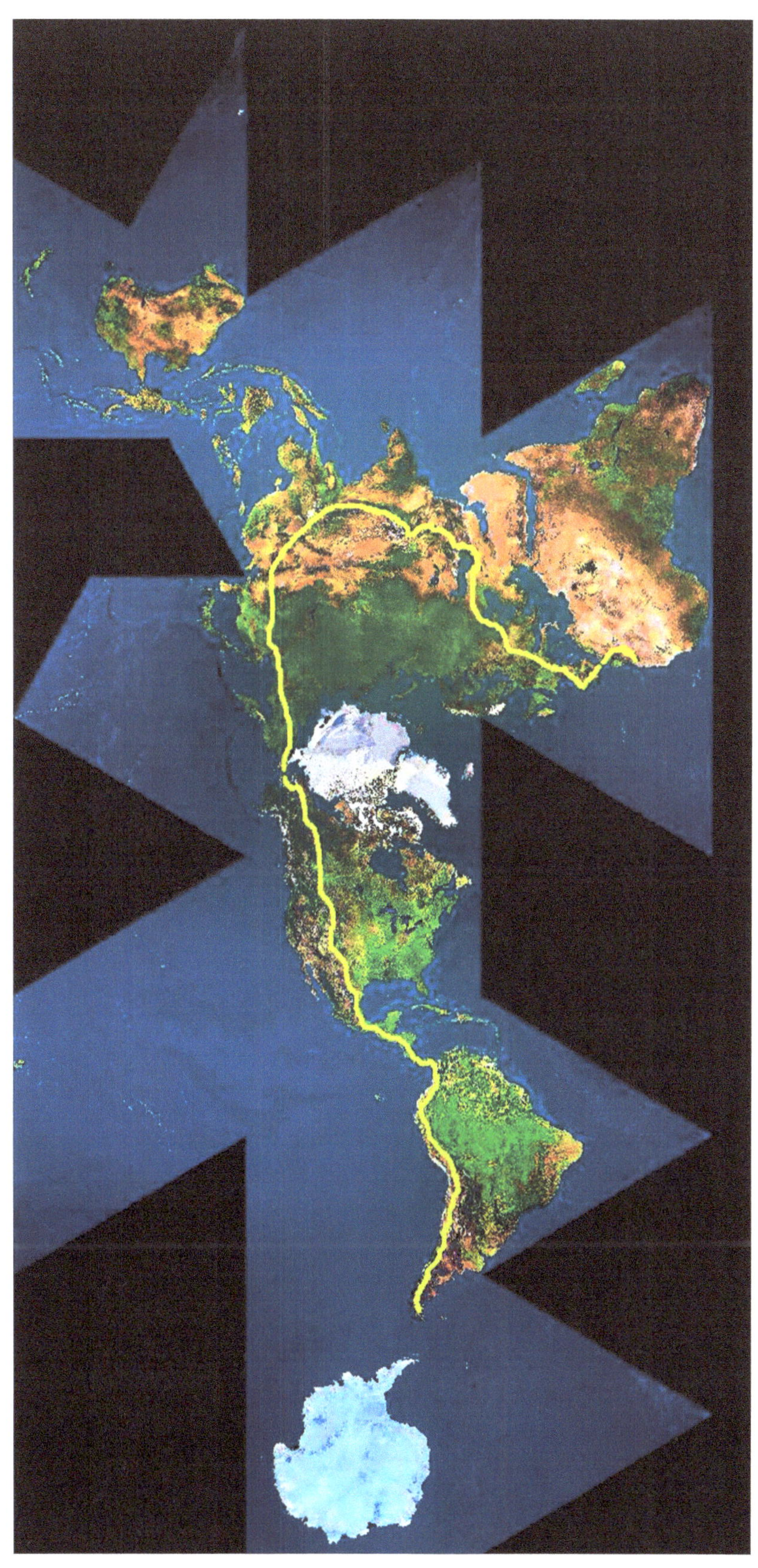

*"A footpath for those seeking fellowship with Earth."*

We need to renegotiate our contract with nature. Ecology is a unifying force that can diminish intolerance and expand our empathy towards others—both human and animal.

Gregory Colbert
*Peace and Harmony: The Message of Our Discovery*


The thing the ecologically illiterate don't realize about an ecosystem is that it's a system. A system! A system maintains a certain fluid stability that can be destroyed by a misstep in just one niche. A system has order, a flowing from point to point. If something dams the flow, order collapses. The untrained miss the collapse until too late. That's why the highest function of ecology is the understanding of consequences.

Frank Herbert
*Dune* ("Appendix I: The Ecology of Dune")


That land is a community is the basic concept of ecology, but that land is to be loved and respected is an extension of ethics.

Aldo Leopold
*A Sand County Almanac*, 01949

# On the Usefulness of
# The International Peace Trail
# to promote and sustain world peace

03/19/02016

There are seven major problems facing the world today: war, hunger, lack of education (ignorance,) poverty, pollution, extinction and disease. Each one has roots and causes in the other and none can find solution in isolation or separate from the whole.

For example, global climate changes have clear links to the destruction of biomass[31]. Biomass is the total mass of living matter within a given unit of environmental area. Believe it or not, biomass is a vital part of our rich cultural heritage. It acts as a whole, like a thermostat, to reduce greenhouse gases, absorb carbon and stabilize the climate into temperate zones supremely suited to life. As we destroy it, we destroy life; as we destroy life, we destroy our home, our heritage and our future.

Clearly everything must begin with conserving and restoring biomass. The *Nature Conservancy* and the *Sierra Club* are excellent examples of organizations working in this area. Please support these groups[32] and others like them[33].

Another example is top-soil. Pedogenesis is the process of soil formation and there is a serious crisis today – the topsoil is disappearing! Soil is a living thing, requiring organic matter to form. But use of chemical pesticides kills these organic components reducing living soil to lifeless dirt and dust. As good soil is lost, plants cannot grow[34] and more biomass is lost.

Thus, organic farming provides direct alternatives to the destruction of biomass through the use of natural methods that preserve and ensure a healthy environment for living soil, the necessary foundation for a healthy biomass and any sustainable system of agriculture[35].

With the restoration of biomass, climate will once again stabilize within a region ideally suited for capturing and distributing the life-sustaining, life-creating properties of the sun. As life flourishes mankind will once again gain reward through the incredible abundance of solar energy distribution in the rich flora and fauna of Earth. As this synergistically produces an increase in biomass, poverty and hunger will gradually diminish.

Also, as many diseases escape the confines of rain forests by excessive logging, a rich biomass will help to isolate and limit the spread of these diseases, Finally, as we are now discovering, many of these diseases lay frozen for thousands of years in what is now rapidly melting Siberian permafrost.

The spread and ravaging effects of disease can also find further reduction by implementing a system of sanitation as proposed by the United Nations. More than 2 million people, mostly children, die every year from diseases caused by lack of sanitation and access to clean drinking water.

As those who involve themselves with these issues[36] can tell you, solving the problem of disease is vital to solving the problem of poverty. So, by providing adequate drinking water and sanitation, the incidence of infant mortality due to disease and poor sanitation can drop as much as 75% according to a UN Study[37]. Again, only by conservation and restoration projects will this be possible.

For example, one of nature's greatest treasures is the aquifer. Aquifers are vital to providing clean water. Believe it or not, many aquifers are being encroached upon and destroyed by rampant development. The aquifer in the Albany Pine Bush, now a landfill for hazardous waste, provides distressing evidence in alarming detail.

Furthermore, as these resources are lost, poverty will increase. It is only by preserving and restoring these areas, by protecting these resources, that we can reduce infant mortality rates due to poor sanitation and dirty drinking water. As infant mortality rates drop, poverty will further diminish, as will issues that bear relation to poverty such as hunger and starvation, crime, war, and the untold suffering and consequences of war.

World peace comes from conservation of wetlands, preservation of aquifers, and the protection of natural habitats. Peace, like life, is synergistic. If you want to fight poverty, you must fight against the causes of poverty as well as its effects. Destroying wetlands impoverishes us all. Rolling over Aquifers in the name of urban sprawl only increases global poverty and disease. Strip mining, mountaintop removal, fracking and slash and burn logging not only increases everyone's risk of disease, these practices limit access to clean water and fresh air and accelerate global climate change[38].

Thus, protecting Earth's diminishing wilderness areas and natural habitats will go a long way toward restoring the biomass which will stabilize the environment and prevent climate change. In all this the International Peace Trail can help!

The International Peace Trail Project envisions a World-Wide Parks and Trails System which will preserve, protect and restore these natural resources and wilderness areas. Such a self-regulating system will work to preserve the diversity of plant and animal life from further encroachment and extinction as well as limit the spread of disease, while protecting and empowering the indigenous tribes and keeping them from poverty and providing a habitat for many endangered species.

By working to solve issues relating to disease and hunger, while providing education and sustainable growth, poverty will diminish whereby further peace will grow and the whole effect will become synergistically self-perpetuating and self-sustaining[39].

It's simple. The creation of the International Peace Trail will help create the world peace that will help create the International Peace Trail[40]. And this in turn will help create world peace!

It seems clear that any solution to the problems of war must first address the problems of poverty, hunger and disease. But before these problems can be addressed, the problems of Earth's dwindling natural resources have to be solved. It all builds upon each other and at the foundation is the extremely rare and precious blue-green marble on which we all live. It simply will not do to address any one of these issues without first addressing the others.

Thus behold the International Peace Trail: it will stretch around the world protecting and linking together wilderness areas, natural habitats, parks and wildlife areas. It will raise awareness and engender support and sponsorship. It will inspire stories and tales that will unify a people.

> Peace is a journey of a thousand miles and it must be taken one step at a time.
>
> Lyndon B. Johnson

The path to an International Peace Trail is through the creation of an International Peace Trail Alliance.

The IPT Alliance will work together with local, state and world governments, the UN, Peace Corp and civil engineers to create the International Peace Trail, which in turn will help link, create, restore and sustain natural habitats and ecosystems through a worldwide parks and trails system.

This system will preserve and protect these lands and resources, restore biomass and bio-diversity, which in turn will reduce global climate change, pollution and the extinction of untold species of plant and animal life. By protecting and restoring these resources, global prosperity will grow. This prosperity will in turn reduce poverty and with it the problems associated with poverty: hunger and disease. And as the problems of hunger and disease are eradicated, so too is poverty!

With the decline of poverty comes the further prosperity of the planet, which in turn will perpetuate the sustainable growth of these habitats and wilderness areas, which in turn will perpetuate further peace and prosperity. It's synergy in action!

With regards pollution, too much of anything is bad and too much $CO_2$ in our upper atmosphere is very bad. When there is robust biomass, $CO_2$ is easily captured by the life-enhancing life-affirming process of photosynthesis, so two things must occur:

1.) We need to cease releasing harmful gases into our air and harmful chemicals into our streams and rivers
2.) We need to capture and remove the tremendous amount of $CO_2$ and other pollutants we have already released.

*Because the effects we are experiencing now are from $CO_2$ released 20-years ago, we still have yet to experience the effects of all the $CO_2$ we have released since then!* Please read that again. Because of years of obfuscation and disinformation stalling action, we have all but foretold our doom. But there are things we can do. Plants are our friend and we need them now more than ever. Clearly, we need to rebuild biomass. As the International Peace Trail envisions a series of trails linking parks, habitats and wilderness areas, it can help by bringing attention to and expanding these areas while helping to create and restore areas around it.

We need to create more parks, plant more tress and remove more pollutants from our global biome. Locally we need to plant more trees, use non-polluting renewable resources, use canvas totes, stop using plastic bags and other disposable non-reusable plastic items. Globally, we need to support such initiatives to restore and rebuild the many diverse and wondrous habitats of nature: rivers and lakes, oceans and coasts, forests and soil, grasslands and prairies, deserts and arid lands, and arctic tundra and high-altitude ecosystems.

The IPT can help focus these projects and expand upon them. In so doing, carbon will be captured and temperatures will return to optimal values for sustaining life. Furthermore, everyone working together to make this happen will engender world peace.

The goal of the International Peace Trail Project is, at first, to promote the idea of the IPT through its website. Then, as interest grows it will hopefully inspire the global will which will eventually form both an International Peace Trail Foundation and the International Peace Trail Alliance.

It will be through the efforts of this alliance that the International Peace Trail will be created and maintained. It will be through the efforts of the International Peace Trail Foundation that an IPT Fund will be created to sustain it.

With the creation of the IPT Alliance, a world-wide parks and trail system will be established, the main corridor of which will be the International Peace Trail. The IPTA will have chapters in every major city of the world. Each Chapter will provide maps and maintain a section of the Trail while providing Internetworking resources to independent groups and organizations dedicated to ecological, biological, geological, and sociological[41] issues. Chapters will become resources for conservation and restoration efforts, ecology and education.

# If you build it,
# peace will come.

If you build it, peace will come. Have you been on the Peace Trail today?

## A brief description of a potential route for the International Peace Trail: A footpath for those seeking fellowship with Earth



**The International Peace Trail** begins atop the **Atlas Mountains** and follows the **IAT** in **Morocco** from Taroudant to Midelt. After a flight in to Casablanca then to Agadir, ascend to Jbel Toubkal(4167) where the trail begins. Follow ridge over Irhil M'Goun (4071) to Jbel Ayachi (3737.) Descend to Midelt follow road to BouLemane and resupply. Ascend ridge to Jbel Bou Naceur (3340) then descend to Taza. Follow ridge to Chaouen, continue on past Tetouan to Ceuta. From Ceuta, cross the Strait of Gibraltar to **Spain**.

**Spain/ France/ Switzerland/Austria/Germany/Hungary**: From Tarifa, join the *E4 - Gibraltar – Pyrenees – Lake Constance – Balaton – Rila – Kreta - Cyprus Trail*. Follow this trail to Bratislava then cross into Slovakia.

> **Alternate Route - Camino de Santiago/Andorra**:  Enter the Parque Natural Del Estrecho and Follow trail to the Huerta Grande Visitors Center. Enter the Parque Natural Los Alcornocales and follow trails to Ubrique. From Ubrique, enter the Sierra de Grazalema Natural Park, follow the A-2302 trail to Rio and follow the CA-9104 trail to Zahara. From Zahara, make for Seville and follow the Camino Mozárabe route of the Camino de Santiago or Way of St. James from Seville to the Cathedral of Santiago de Compostela in Galicia. Follow the Camino Francés route to the Chemin d'Arles or Voie d'Arles route to Jaca. From Jaca ascend El Turbon (2492), continue over Cotiella (2912), Mtes Malditos (3404)and Pic d'Estats (3141), following the French-Spanish Border. Pass through **Andorra** to the border of **France** and join the E4 Trail.

> **Alternate Route - Monaco/France/Italy/Switzerland/Liechtenstein/ Germany/ Austria/Slovenia - Via Alpina:**  Depart E4 trail and make way to Monaco and the beginning of the Via Alpina "network" of five long-

distance hiking trails. Continue to Austria then rejoin the E4 Trail to Bratislava.

**Slovakia/Ukraine**: Make way to Banska Bystrica. Ascend Dumbier (2043) continue on to Tatry (2655) and the Carpathian Mountains. Follow Slovakian-Polish border to Ukrainian border. Enter Ukraine Make way through Romania and Moldova to Odesa. Follow roads through Mykolayiv, Kherson, Dzhankoy, Simferopol, Sudak, Feodosiya, Kerch. Make way to Sochi. Enter the Caucusus Mountains and ascend Elbrus (5642). Continue over Dykh Tau (5203), Shkhara (5201), Uilpata (4638), Kazbek (5047), Argun (4494), Diklosmta (4276), and Gora (4466). Enter **Azerbaijan**, descend to Baki. Follow road to Astara, cross border into **Iran**

**Iran/Afghanistan/Pakistan/India**: Follow roads through Rasht, Ghaem Shahr, Sari, Gorgan, Bojnurd, and Quchan, to Mashhad. Cross border into **Afghanistan**. Make way to Herat, enter the **Hindu Kush**. Pass through Nayak, enter Kuh-e Baba region, ascend Shah Fuladi (5143).Descend to Farakhulm and make way to Kabul. Follow roads through Sarowbi and Jalalabad to Khyber Pass and the border to **Pakistan**. Follow roads through Nowshera, Dargai, Mongoba, and Drosh to Chitral. Ascend Tirich Mir (7690) and continue over Sad Istragh (7367), and Lunkho (6901.) Descend to Vakhan. Follow roads through Langar, and Buzai Gumbad to Mingteke. Make way to Mazar. Ascend to Aghil Pass and enter the **Karakoram Range**. Continue to K2 (8611) and border of **India**. Continue to Gasherbraum (8068) and Masherbraum (7821). Descend to Parkutta. Follow roads through Marol, Kargil, Nurla, Sutak, Kibar, Dankhar and Sangnam to Kalpa. Enter the **Himalayas** and ascend to Nilang. Ascend Gangotri (6614),continue over Kedarnath Pk. (6940),and Badrinath Pks ( 7068). Descend to Mana. Ascend Kamet (7756), continue to Nanda Devi (7816), and Trisul (7127). Descend to Askot and ascend to Api (7132). Descend to Darma pass and border to **China**.

**China/Tibet/Nepal**: Follow roads through Barang and Barga to Darchen. Circumambulate **Mt. Kailash** 14 times. Return to Barang. Follow roads to border of **Nepal**. Continue through Simikot, Galwa, and Jumla to Tibrikot. Ascend Dhaulagiri (8167) and descend to Tukche. Ascend Annapurna ( 8091) and descend to Pokhara. Follow roads to Kathmandu. Turn prayer wheels at **Swayambhunath**. Follow road to Namche Bazar and ascend **Mt. Everest** (8848). Pay respects to **Chomolungma**. Make way to Mt. Makalu (8463) and descend to Flatia. Ascend Kangchenjunga (8586) and descend to Mangan. Follow roads through Gagtok and Yadong to Thimphu. Ascend Chomo Lhari

(7313) and descend to Guru. Follow roads through Qonggyai, Nedong, and Nang to Qabnag. Ascend Namoha Barwa (7756) and descend to Wulang. Follow roads through Kangri Karpo Pass, Rawu, Baxoi, Zogang, Markam, Chubalung, Batang, Litang, and Yajiang to Kangding. Ascend Gongga Shan (7514) and descend to Tianguan. Follow roads through Ya'an, Chengdu, Deyang, Mianyangi, Guangyuan, Hanzhong, Xi'an, Luo Yang, and Shijiazhuang to Beijing. Continue through Shenyang, Changchun, Harbin, and Bei'an to border of **Russian Federation**.

**Russian Federation**: From Blagoveshchensk follow roads through Tynda, Yakutsk, and Orotukan to Omsukchan. Make way through Khrebet Kolymskiy region, Evensk, Gizhiga, Ust'Penzhirro, Kamenskoye, Penzhino, Markovo, Otrozhnyy, Uel'Kal, Egvekinot, and Lul'tin to Vankarem. Cross Bering Stait to **North American Continent**.

**North American Continent**: From Point Hope in Alaska, enter the **Brooks Range**. Follow Delong Mountains through Endicott Mountains to Philip Smith Mts. Descend to Stevens Village. Follow roads through Fairbanks to Anderson. Ascend Mt Hayes ( 4216) and continue over Wrangell Mts. to St. Elias Mts. Enter **Canada** and Yukon Territory. Ascend Mt. Logan (6050) and descend to Haines Junction. Follow roads through Whitehorse and Teslin Lake to Border of British Columbia. Follow roads to Toad River. Ascend Mt. Roosevelt(2972), Churchill Pk. (2819), Mt. Stalin (2819), Mt. Sylvia (2972) and Great Snow Mountain. (2896). Descend to Sikanni Chief. Follow roads through Pink Mountain, Fort St. John, and Dawson Creek to Tumbler Ridge. Ascend Sentinel Pk. (2515), continue over Mt. Sir Alexander (3279). Descend to Border of Alberta. Pass through Willmore Wilderness Prov. Park and ascend Mt. Chown (3331). Continue over Mt Robson (3954) and enter **Mt. Robson Prov. Park**. Continue to **Jasper National Park** and ascend Mt. Edith Cavell (3363), Mt. Alberta (3619), and Mt. Columbia (3747). Pass through Rocky Mountains Forest Preserve, Yono Nat. Park, Kootenay Nat. Park, and ascend Mt. Assiniboine (3618), Mt. Joffre (3449), and Mt. Lyall (2950). Pass through Waterton Lakes Nat. Park and the Waterton-Glacier **International Peace Park** and continue to border of the **United States** and the **Continental Divide Trail (CDT)**. Enter Glacier Nat. Park and follow the CDT though the Lewis Range. Descend to Helena. Cross the Absaroka range and ascend Gannet Peak (4202). Descend to Lander. Continue through Medicine Bow Mts to Rawlins Pass. Continue through Mt. Zirkel Wilderness, Never Summer Wilderness, Rocky Mountain National Park, Indian Peaks Wilderness, Vasquez Wilderness, Holy Cross Wilderness, Mt Massive Wilderness, and

Collegiate Peaks Wilderness. Descend to Monarch Pass. Continue through Lagarita Wilderness to Weminuche Wilderness and descend to Cumbres Pass. Ascend Wheeler Peak (4011) and descend to Taos. Make way to Tsoddzil, the Turquoise Mountain and ascend. Return to the CDT and follow to the border of Mexico. Follow Sierra Madre Occidental to S. Pablo. Ascend Atlacomulco (3633) and descend to Mexico City. Ascend Nevado de Toluca (4577) and **Popocatepetl** (5452) and descend to Peublo. Follow roads to border of **Guatemala**.

**Central and South America**: Make way through **Guatemala, Salvador, Honduras, Nicaragua, Costa Rica**, and **Panama**, to **Columbia**. From the border enter the **Andes Mountains**. Follow roads through Mendellin to Sonson and ascend ridge. Follow ridge to N.del Ruiz (5399). Descend to Ibague. Continue along ridge through Parque Nacional Las Hermsas and ascend N.del Auila (5750). Continue over Volcan de Purnace (4686) and descend to Popayan. Follow roads through Pasto to Tuquerres. Ascend N. de Cumbal (4764) and descend to border of **Ecuador**. Enter the **Ecuadoran Andes** Follow road though Tulcan to Ibarra. Ascend Volcan Cayambe (5790) and continue over Co Antisana (5704), Vol Cotopaxi (5896), and descend to Latacunga. Follow roads through Cuenca and Saraguro to Loja. Pass through Parque Nacional Podocarpus. Continue to border of **Peru**, enter the **Peruvian Andes**. Follow roads through San Ignacio to Jaen. Pass through Parque Nacional Curervo. Follow roads through Huambos, Chotta, Cajamarca, and Corongo to Huaylas. Ascend Nev. de Huascaran (6768) and pass through Parque Nacional Huascaran. Ascend Yerupaja (6634) and descend to Huanuco. Follow roads through Ayacucho, and Ahuaylas to Antabambo. Pass through Cord de Huanzo and discover source of Amazon River. Continue over Nev de Ampato (6310), Nev de Chachani (6075) and El Misti (5822). Descend to Arequipa and follow roads through Omate, Moquegua, Llo and Tacnia to border of **Chile** and the **Chilean Andes**. Ascend Vol. Tacora (5988) and descend to Lagos. Follow road to Charana and border of Bolivia. Enter Parque Nac. Luaca and ascend Nev Sajama (6542), Guallatiri (6060), Co Cabaraya (5869), Sillajhuay (5998). Descend to Lilicia. Follow roads through Julacia, to Ollague. Ascend Co Aucanquilcha (5118) and descend to Calama. Ascend Vol Licancabur (5921), and Co Zapaleri (5655). Follow border of **Argentina** over Co del Rincon (5594),Co Pular (6225) and descend to Socompa. Ascend Vol Llullaillaro (6723), Vol Anotfalla (6440), Sanevada (6400) and descend to Paso de San Francisco. Ascend Ojos del Salado (6908), Vol Copiapo (6080) and descend to La Guardia. Pass through Paso de Pena Negra and ascend Co de Petro (5830). Descend to Paso del Inea and ascend Co de Toro (6380), Co

Las Tortolas (6332), Co del Olivares (6282), Ollitas (5620), Co Merrecedario (6770), Co Aconeagua (6960), Juncal (6060), Cerro Tupungato (5682), Vol San Jose (5830), Vol Maipo (5390)Sosneado P. de las Damas (5160), Vol Peteroa (4090), Co Mora (3650), Campanario (4020) and descend to Banos Maule. Make way to Parque Nac. Laguna de Laja, ascend Vol Copahue (2969). Pass through Parque Nac. Tolhuaca, Parque Nac. Villarrica, Parque Nac. Nahue and ascend Ventisquerro (2300). Pass through Parque Nac. Los Alerces, Parque Nac. Quellat and descend to Simpson. Enter Valentin Parque Nac. ascend Monte San Valentin (4058), continue to San Rafael and descend to San Carlos. Make way through the Parque Nac. Bernardo O'Higgins and **Parque Nac. Los Glaciares to the Parque Nac. Torres del Paine** and the end of the **IPT**. Depart from Puerto Natales.

.

*Appendix B*

## A Simple formula for peace

$$☮ = ♥☺^2$$

☮ = peace, freedom from disturbance; quiet restfulness and tranquility; harmony.

♥ = love, a state characterized by care, consideration and compassion; empathy.

☺ = happiness, a state characterized by pleasure, contentment, or enduring and abiding joy.

$☮ = ♥☺^2$ means peace equals love times happiness-squared.

Paradoxically, happiness by itself, or solely for oneself, $☺^1$, does not lead to happiness. It may seem to at first but in fact concern only for one's own wellbeing will only ever lead to restlessness and misery, $☺^0$.

And it will never lead to peace in life.

True happiness comes from happiness-squared; from caring for others, from concerning yourself with someone or something other than yourself, from service and stewardship, from spreading joy and goodwill, from participating in something larger, from community and faith. Happiness by itself is consumptive and zero-sum, it eventually eats itself; happiness-squared, in contrast, is productive and non-zero sum, it increases wealth and prosperity for everyone.

But it cannot achieve lasting peace without love.

By itself, happiness-squared results in fractional unity, many splintering groups or sects set upon themselves, unable to achieve peace outside of their own special interests, groups, clans, tribes, councils or committees. By itself it perpetuates a system of haves and have-nots and this cannot lead to lasting peace. But when happiness squared is multiplied by love, out of many comes one and from this is forged the foundation for building lasting and sustainable world peace.

*     *     *

Formula for peace: ☮=♥☺²

☮ = peace, freedom from war; sustained calm and tranquility; harmony.
♥ = love, a state characterized by care, compassion and consideration; empathy.
☺ = happiness, a state characterized by satisfaction, contentment, or enduring and abiding joy.

☮=♥☺² means peace equals love times happiness squared.

Happiness squared means caring about others, sharing in their joys and spreading good will, regardless of opposing affiliation, difference or indifference. It means the greatest act of selfishness is selflessness and it works on the basic fundamental principle that a rising tide raises all ships. It means, treat others with dignity and respect because "The King will reply, 'Truly I tell you, whatever you did for one of the least of these brothers and sisters of mine, you did for me.'" Matthew 25:40

But our most immediate concern, our current plight, is that there is no longer a sustainable path to the future in a world where there is no peace. Spreading good will without love leads to sectarianism, division; and this invariably leads to conflict and war. But when we can learn to be inclusive, when our decisions include everyone, when everyone's success is shared by everyone else and no one is left behind, then at last we can begin to develop sustainable methods of ensuring lasting peace and tranquility. Both our long-term survival on Earth and our smooth transition to an interplanetary species depend on it.

Thus, peace equals love times happiness squared.

*     *     *

What is happiness squared? It means caring about others, sharing in their joys and spreading good will, regardless of opposing affiliation, difference or indifference. It means the greatest act of selfishness is selflessness and it works on the basic fundamental principle that a rising tide raises all ships.

Because the rewards of everyone's happiness are a millionfold greater than any happiness we could ever hope to achieve alone, by devoting ourselves to the happiness of others we inevitably help ourselves far more than we ever could simply by only helping ourselves.

But the deeper truth is that true happiness only comes from helping others, by making others happy! We may think otherwise but with wisdom we see that when we only concern ourselves with our own happiness, we never truly find it! Such a happiness is an illusion and because it is an illusion it actually leads to misery, not happiness. No, true happiness can only come from happiness squared. Indeed, in our ever increasingly integrated world, there can be no happiness for ourselves unless it includes everyone. Gone are the days that our happiness can be at anyone else's expense. We must learn to co-evolve together or die.

But more importantly, without love times happiness squared there can be no lasting or sustainable peace! When we learn to be inclusive, when our decisions include everyone, when everyone's success is dependent upon everyone else's and no one is left behind, then at last we can begin to develop sustainable methods of ensuring our long-term survival on the only planet we've got! Once we realize this, peace becomes of paramount importance as there can be no sustainable future without it.

Thus, peace equals love times happiness squared.


'Truly I tell you, whatever you did for one of the least of
these brothers and sisters of mine, you did for me.'

Matthew 25:40-45

http://www.sierraclub.org/

http://www.worldwildlife.org/home-full.html

http://www.rainforest-alliance.org/

http://www.npca.org/

http://www.worldlandtrust.org/

http://www.who.int/en/

http://www.unicef.org/index.php

http://www.foodforthepoor.org/

http://www.cdtrail.org/page.php

http://www.iat-sia.org/index.php

http://worldtrailsnetwork.org/

https://www.crs.org/

To know now what we could never have known before [0]1969—that we now have an option for all humanity to "make it" successfully on this planet in this lifetime—is not to be optimistic. It is only a validation of hope, a hope that had no operationally foreseeable validity before [0]1969. Whether it is to be Utopia or Oblivion will be a touch-and-go relay race right up to the final moment. The race is between a better-informed, hopefully inspired young world versus a running-scared, misinformedly brain-conditioned, older world. Humanity is in "final exam" as to whether or not it qualifies for continuance in Universe…

R. Buckminster Fuller
*Critical Path, 01981*

Notes:

---

<sup></sup>

[1] https://quoteinvestigator.com/2013/01/22/borrow-earth/
[2] Perhaps the book can be summed up by a few short words from the book's introduction. "Neither the great political and financial power structures of the world, nor the specialization-blinded professionals, nor the population in general realize that sum-totally the omni-engineering-integratable, invisible revolution in the metallurgical, chemical, and electronic arts now makes it possible to do so much more with ever fewer pounds and volumes of material, ergs of energy, and seconds of time per given technological function that it is now highly feasible to take care of everybody on Earth at a 'higher standard of living than any have ever known.' It no longer has to be you or me. Selfishness is unnecessary and henceforth unrationalizable as mandated by survival. War is obsolete... It is a matter of converting the high technology from weaponry to livingry." (pg. xxv)
[3] This is not easy as studies show people would rather make $50,000 if everyone else is making only $25,000 than make $100,000 if everyone else is making $250,000!
http://www.michaelshermer.com/2008/01/weird-things-about-money/

The sad truth is it seems no one wants to be a billionaire if everyone is a billionaire. There is obviously then an aspect of capitalism that is less about money and more about vanity and prestige, status and power. In short capitalism is often more about ego than commerce. But worse, capitalism has no moral component, no conscience beyond increasing shareholder value. To be successful in business, you must only care about profits, which is to say serves only Mammon.

There is so much more to say on this subject, it could fill a book! The problem is, much of the world enjoys its luxuries at the expense of someone else. We all agree, regardless of cause or who is to blame, many people fall through the cracks or are unable or unwilling to pull themselves up from where they land. In an age when wealth and technology should be able to solve these problems back when Fuller is alive, the statistics on poverty are staggering! The fact that in spite of wealth and technology these problems remain, shows there are other forces at work here. And that is the true evil of our days. These are the powers-that-be that Jesus rails against!

> Again I say to you, it is easier for a camel to go through the eye of a needle, than for a rich man to enter the kingdom of God.

Matthew 19:24

The fact is, there *is* enough for everyone; we don't need to exploit one another. The fact is, we don't need to perpetuate a system of haves and have-nots, when there is abundance for all. **The fact is, we receive more energy from the sun in an hour than the entire world consumes in a year!**

The problem is, solar power breaks the system of exploitation by providing abundance for all. This is why we refuse to develop space-based solar power and insist on waging war for oil rather than fund a solar/renewal energy revolution, because people would rather be poor if everyone else is poorer, than rich if everyone else is richer, or at least as rich.

> If the rich could hire other people to die for them, the poor could make a wonderful living.

> Yiddish Proverb
> from The Wisdom and Wit of Rabbi Jesus by William E. Phipps

The problem is entrenched through income inequality. The fact is, the greatest increase in income inequality since feudalism has happened during this generation. The question is, who benefits from the fruits of those who have stood on the backs on giants? Should the benefits of advances in technology, specifically with regards automation, only uplift the boats of a few or should they uplift all boats?

> "If machines produce everything we need, the outcome will depend on how things are distributed. Everyone can enjoy a life of luxurious leisure if the machine-produced wealth is shared, or most people can end up miserably poor if the machine-owners successfully lobby against wealth redistribution. So far, the trend seems to be toward the second option, with technology driving ever-increasing inequality."

> Stephen Hawking
> https://www.reddit.com/r/science/comments/3nyn5i/science_ama_series_s tephen_hawking_ama_answers/cvsdmkv

"The Sun delivers more energy to Earth in an hour than we use in a year…"
http://www.sandia.gov/~jytsao/Solar%20FAQs.pdf

"The total solar energy absorbed by Earth's atmosphere, oceans and land masses is approximately 3,850,000 exajoules (EJ) per year. In 2002, this was more energy in one hour than the world uses in one year."
https://en.wikipedia.org/wiki/Solar_energy#cite_ref-Smil_1991_5-0

Powering the planet: Chemical challenges in solar energy utilization
http://www.pnas.org/content/103/43/15729.full.pdf

Every hour, more solar energy reaches the Earth than humans use in a year.
http://energy.gov/articles/space-based-solar-power

[4] Indeed, it is cooperation (or more specifically co-evolution, which is a natural consequence of cooperation) which has brought life in Earth to where it is today. Without it, humanity would never have made it out of the stone ages, let alone out of the ocean! For example, if poor farming practices resulted in the death of all plankton in the ocean, we would die as well, as that is the source of over 2/3rds the planet's oxygen. Thus, from a global perspective, we must cooperate with plankton. We cannot live without it.

Co-evolution is the product of cooperation over time. A classic example can be found in the Albany Pine Bush. Through a process of co-evolution over thousands of years, the Karner Blue Butterfly (Lycaeides melissa samuelis) has developed a mutually supportive relationship with a small flower known as Blue Lupine (Lupinus perennis.) Due to a reciprocal evolutionary exchange which can only be described as cooperative, the butterfly has developed a symbiotic relationship with the flower! The butterfly aids in the pollination of the blue lupine and likewise, the flower serves as both food and shelter to the eggs of the butterfly. Indeed, without the blue lupine, the Karner Blue would not survive.

Currently, due to urban development, the Karner Blue is on the Endangered Species list. Unfortunately, the problem is there are currently no laws to protect endangered ecosystems. But there are laws protecting endangered species. Thus, there are several organizations that are working to save habitats and ecosystems, such as *The Nature Conservancy* and *Save the Pine Bush*, who use the endangered Karner Blue butterfly as the legal basis for their lawsuits to save the Pine Bush and habitats like it. For more information, please visit: http://www.savethepinebush.org/KB/KB_Index.html or the New York State Department of Environmental Conservation, on the web at:
http://www.dec.state.ny.us/website/dfwmr/wildlife/endspec/kbbufs.html

[5] One could call it Bucky's bible, but that moniker might be better suited to his other more massive and mind-blowing work, *Synergetics*. Perhaps this impossible to describe work can be adequately summed up by a few quotes from its considerable introduction:

> "Only a comprehensive switch from the narrowing specialization and toward an ever more inclusive and refining comprehension by all humanity – regarding all the factors governing omnicontinuing life aboard our spaceship Earth – can bring about reorientation from the self-extinction-bound human trending, and do so within the critical time remaining before we have passed the point of chemical process irretrievably." *Synergetics*, pg. xxvii

> "Advancing science has now discovered that all the known cases of biological extinction have been caused by overspecialization, whose concentration of only selected genes sacrifices general adaptability." pg. xxv

> "Each age is characterized by its own astronomical myriads of new, special-case experiences and problems to be stored in freshly born optimum capacity human brains — which storages in turn may disclose to human minds the presence of heretofore undiscovered, unsuspectedly existent eternal generalized principles." *ibid*, pg. xiv

> "We are now synergetically forced to conclude that all phenomena are
> metaphysical; wherefore, as many have long suspected - like it or not - life
> is but a dream." pg. xxxi

The book then begins to generalize from basic geometric principles to reach some
amazing and quite mind-blowing generalizations:

> "Unity is plural and, at minimum, is two." 224.12, pg. 54

> "The explicable requires the inexplicable. Experience requires the
> nonexperienceable. The obvious requires the mystical. This is a powerful
> group of paired concepts generated by the complementarity of
> conceptuality." 501.13, pg. 222

> "Truth is cosmically total: synergetic. Verities are generalized principles
> stated in semimetaphorical terms. Verities are differentiable. But love is
> omniembracing, omnicoherent, and omni-inclusive, *with no
> exceptions.* Love, like synergetics, is nondifferentiable, i.e., is integral."
> 1005.54, pg. 619

> "The highest of generalizations is the synergetic integration of truth and
> love." 1005.56, pg. 619.

[6] If you knew just how often life defies the odds, you might have inclination to believe we
are the most improbable creatures in Universe. Indeed, only the luckiest survive.

First, there is the Anthropic Principle. Quite simply, if we weren't the luckiest creatures,
to live in a universe so precisely tuned as to allow for us to exist, we wouldn't be here to
marvel at just how lucky we are! Sounds pretty obvious until you find out just how
precisely tuned Universe really is and how even the slightest deviation of say the weight
of hydrogen, would render a universe in which life could not exist because stars could not
form. And as we all contain elements that could not have been created without many older
stars going super-nova, (we are literally the stuff of stars) we would not be here today. So,
the precise weight of hydrogen is one of many cosmological constants ideally suited to a
universe ideally suited to life ideally suited to contemplating this fact!

In the universe there are several other precise tunings which are called dimensionless
physical constants. That is, universal physical constants such as pi or phi which are entirely
independent of arbitrary systems of units or measurements. Any suitably intelligent life-
form will eventually discover them. Currently it is said man has discovered some 26
fundamental constants.
http://www.math.ucr.edu/home/baez/constants.html

It is likely more will be discovered when physics learns more about the nature of dark
matter, dark energy and perhaps even dark time, assuming they are not simply an attempt
to explain away the hidden structure of Universe and its incompatibility with current

scientific theories. Basically, 'What if the discrepancy arises from a flaw in our theory of gravity rather than from some provider of mass that we cannot see?'
http://www.scientificamerican.com/article/dark-matter-modified-gravity/

Another aspect to the precisely tuned nature of Universe is in the relationships *between* constants. For example, gravity is approximately $10^{39}$ times weaker than the electromagnetic force. If gravity were any weaker "stars would be a billion times less massive and would burn a million times faster" and would not produce enough of the higher elements necessary for truly advanced forms of life.

Other fascinating properties of the universe include the relation of the nuclear weak force to gravity. Had the weak force been any weaker, "all the hydrogen in the universe would have been turned to helium (making water impossible…")
http://ourworld.compuserve.com/homepages/rossuk/c-anthro.htm

Then there is the whole concept of Darwinian Evolution. It is like living in a universe where only heads are flipped. In the space of all universes, this space is still infinite. However, each instance in which tails are rolled is an instance where some genetic deviation, some unfortunate miscalculation or random mutation, didn't survive. We have lived so far in a world, thanks to Darwinian Evolution, where only the strong, only the heads, survive.

Furthermore, there are the special properties of carbon and water, the mathematical precision of protein-folding, the manner in which amino acids link together to form proteins, etc.

Carbon forms the basis of all organic life as we know it. Through a process called *catenation*, carbon is able to bond with itself, leading to enormous versatility and usefulness. More compounds are formed with carbon than with any other element.

Water possesses a special property rare in nature. So far as we know, most all matter becomes heavier, denser, when it moves from a gaseous to a liquid and then solid state. One notable and very important exception is water. Water forms a lattice, which expands as heat is removed, making it lighter as a solid than as a liquid (its density decreases by about 9%.) Without this special property, ice would sink and the world would be in a perpetual ice age unconducive to complex warm-blooded life. Furthermore, water is ideally suited to evaporative cooling. Indeed, the ability of water to remove surface heat through evaporation is more effective that alcohol. In humans, through perspiration, this value is 576cal/g, whereas alcohol has a value of 237cal/g. This means water removes 339cal/g more heat from the skin's surface than does alcohol!
http://www.dummies.com/how-to/content/the-unusual-properties-of-water-molecules.html
http://chemwiki.ucdavis.edu/Physical_Chemistry/Physical_Properties_of_Matter/Bulk_Properties/Unusual_Properties_of_Water

Proteins possess an enormous space of possibility with regard to folding, which is the process by which a polypeptide chain folds to form a 3-dimentsional shape necessary for its proper function. Conventional computers require large amounts of time to compute the correct shape. Yet proteins possess an ability to fold spontaneously, showing seemingly hidden knowledge as to their correct configuration prior to folding.

There is an excellent examination of the wealth of evidence for biological design in the book *Nature's Design* by Michael J. Denton. Say what you will about the provocative conclusions he draws, the book is a *tour de force* of the vast if not well-known scientific evidence pointing to design and purpose in Life, the Universe and Everything. Whether you believe the evidence of design as detailed in his book is proof of God or not, one thing seems clear: the universe is exquisitely fine-tuned to develop complex self-replicating information-processing biological systems of great diversity and beauty. Furthermore, the universe is exquisitely fine-tuned to develop creatures capable of recognizing just how exquisitely fine-tuned it is!

It should be noted, to those who disparage the theory of evolution, that the mechanism of natural selection is much like following a script and thus one may ask from whom or from what does this script arise? If we apply Occam's Razor, which is the simpler explanation: that there is a powerful sentient force which exists outside of Universe and which precisely tunes the universal constants to make them ideally suited for life or that there exists a perhaps infinite number of universes in which each these constants vary and in which, for the vast majority, sentient life does not and cannot exist? Thus, evolution constitutes proof of the existence of God.

Another aspect which should be mentioned is the work done in the field of non-linear thermodynamics, specifically with dissipative structures. It would seem both mind and mankind-as-a-whole act like dissipative structures. The salient point is that they are far from equilibrium but rather than crash they move even farther from equilibrium. In other words, they are unstable but, counterintuitively, instead of falling to a point of greater stability, they instead move to a state of greater *instability*. Dissipative structures seem to be all about defying the odds!

Finally, there is something called Quantum Immortality. This is a variation of a thought experiment called Quantum Suicide, which is basically the Schrödinger's cat experiment but from the cat's perspective. It is based on the many-worlds interpretation of quantum mechanics, as put forth by Hugh Everett, which states basically that, at the quantum level, everything that can happen does happen. From this is born the idea of the multiverse, the realm of all possible universes and all possible events within them.

The theory of quantum immortality states that, as the wave function collapses, consciousness chooses to select and therefore exist within universes in which the wave function will not or has not yet collapsed or has fallen on the side in which, from the perspective of being within the box, the cat is still alive. From the cat's perspective, this is tantamount to living a blessed life. However, much like the Anthropic Principle, this is simply because we would not be around to notice otherwise. But this is also the great blessing because, thank God we are!

Ilya Prigogine, Chaos, and Dissipative Structures
 http://www.osti.gov/accomplishments/prigogine.html

The Phenomenology of Dissipative/Replicative Structures
http://edgeoforder.org/pofdisstruct.html

Quantum Mechanics and Immortality
http://www.damninteresting.com/quantum-mechanics-and-immortality/
[7] While we may live in a four-dimensional space-time continuum, in our minds and on computers we may construct fifth dimensional hyperspaces and study fourth dimensional matrixes. In this way we may sometimes see ahead of and around corners, or at least around "ensembles" of corners. If indeed we can see the future, then it is just a matter of tracing it back through the labyrinth of time and space to where we are now and moving forward from there. Good luck!

Also, nonlinear thermodynamics of the kind pioneered by Ilya Prigogine, shows us that far from equilibrium strange and wondrous things are possible. Dissipative Structures represent a paradoxical movement from instability to greater instability; an example of which would be our civilization, poised as it is on the brink of destruction either through nuclear annihilation or ecological catastrophe.

Finally, in response to Fermi's Paradox (see next note,) it may well be that no dissipative structure is capable of becoming a Type 1 civilization. This needs to be proven wrong but so far as we know, no one has done so!
[8] But will *we*? The **Fermi Paradox** suggests that perhaps we will not! The Fermi Paradox essentially asks, "Where are all the aliens?" Why do we seem so alone in Universe when, according to even the most conservative applications of the Drake equation (see below,) the Universe should be teeming with intelligent life? So, where is it? The Fermi Paradox basically suggests that there is some sort of wall or barrier, a *ring-pass-not*, which prevents the emergence of type 1 civilizations, as defined by the Kardashev scale.

Proposed in 01964 by Soviet astronomer Nikolai Kardashev, the **Kardashev Scale** is a method of classifying the technological level of a civilization with regard to the amount of useable energy it has at its disposal. A type I or *Interplanetary* civilization is able to utilize the entire energy resources of a single planet, approximately $10^{16}$ W or more of power. A type II, or *Interstellar* civilization is able to utilize approximately $10^{26}$ W or more of power, the total energy of a single star, and a type III, or *Intergalactic* civilization has at its disposal approximately $10^{36}$ W or more of power, the total energy available from a single galaxy!
http://en.wikipedia.org/wiki/Kardashev_scale

Michio Kaku, popular theoretical physicist, author, and co-founder of string field theory then asks, well it's certainly been long enough, where are all the type I, II, and III cultures? And as far as we can see, there aren't any. If we make it to type I, as far as we know, we will be the first. And he asks why this is and concludes that it is a very dangerous period, the transition from a type 0 civilization to a type I and that so far, at least within our local universe, no one seems to have made it.

> "Given the fact that astrophysicists do not see evidence of life in nearby star systems, even though Drake's equations predict the existence of thousands of intelligent civilizations in our galaxy, it is possible that our galaxy is filled with the ruins of Type 0 civilizations which either settled old grudges via element 92 or else uncontrollably polluted their planet."

Michio Kaku, *Visions* (01997) Anchor Books pg. 324

*    *    *

The **Drake Equation** provides an approximate measure of intelligent life that should theoretically exist in Cosmos given certain basic assumptions or variables.

$N = R^* \, f_p \, n_e \, f_l \, f_i \, f_c \, L$, where $N$ = the number of civilizations capable of communicating with other possible civilizations. Visit SETI League.org to learn what the other variables are.
http://www.setileague.org/general/drake.htm

However, in answer to Mr. Kaku, we would humbly suggest another variable called S, where S = synergy. Where no other type 0 or type 1 civilizations exist nearby, the chance of a type 0 civilization becoming a type 1 is near zero. However, if there *are* other type 0 or type 1 civilizations nearby, then the synergy approaches 1, that a type 0 civilization will become a type 1. Two nearby competing races could conceivably find peace and work together to become type 1 civilizations and of course, the same goes for type 2 and type 3 civilizations. Indeed, according to Synergy, that is the only way type 3 civilizations can exist. It is cooperation, not competition, that makes life both possible and sustainable in Universe.

Update: I have most recently learned (10/25/02016) that Fermi's paradox is not a paradox nor it is Fermi's!
https://blogs.scientificamerican.com/guest-blog/the-fermi-paradox-is-not-fermi-s-and-it-is-not-a-paradox/
That said, the article clearly states:

> "According to these eyewitnesses, they were chatting about a cartoon in The New Yorker showing cheerful aliens emerging from a flying saucer carrying trash cans stolen from the streets of New York City, and Fermi asked "Where is everybody?"

So, take it as you will.
[9] Alternate translation: is given a message from *The Holy Spirit*.

Actually, the longer story here is that the germ of the idea emerges from a quip made by President Reagan in a speech before the United Nations in 01987: "I occasionally think how quickly our differences worldwide would vanish if we were facing an alien threat from outside this world…"

Obviously, this is not a practical means of uniting the planet. But what about something else, is there anything *besides* an alien invasion that might unite us? It is from this strange confluence that many years later the idea for a Peace Trail arises.

[10] One such example can be found on my first trip to Paris. At the top of the Eiffel Tower, I hear someone speaking English. I say, hey you're Americans! Where're you from? They say New York. I say, I'm from New York, upstate near Albany. They say yes, near Albany. I say, Loudonville. They say, yes. Loudonville! I say, when home on leave, I live on S-- Rd; they say they live one block away on J-- Lane!

[11] I will always have a special place in my heart for Ed Seagroatt and Seagroatt-Riccardi. Please visit http://www.seagroattriccardi.com/ and tell them Düg Fresh sent you!

[12] Or at the very least, do no harm.

[13] There is a tendency, among the Baby Boomers, to want to blame the Millennials for much of the problems facing us today. But we have seen more wealth concentrated into hands of the top .01% in the last 50-years than ever before.  We've seen the greatest reduction in wildlife populations in roughly the same amount of time. The millennials cannot be blamed for this. Sadly, most of the blame belongs with the Boomers for selfishly squandering the riches of their forefathers and then ruthlessly grabbing more, gutting everything in their path to fill an insatiable greed.

> "The world has enough for everyone's need, but not enough for everyone's greed."
>
> Mahatma Gandhi.

[14] www.peacetrail.org

[15] Forests and climate change Carbon and the greenhouse effect
http://www.fao.org/docrep/005/ac836e/AC836E03.htm
"Planting new forests, rehabilitating degraded forests and enriching existing forests contribute to mitigating climate change as these actions increase the rate and quantity of carbon sequestration in biomass."

Not just recycled sunlight: Biomass burning and its influence on global climate change
https://www.iop.org/activity/groups/subject/env/prize/file_52569.pdf

Deforestation Facts - What is Deforestation? | NRDC
http://www.nrdc.org/energy/forestsnotfuel/

Forests and Climate Change – UNEP
http://www.unep.org/training/programmes/Instructor%20Version/Part_2/Activities/External_Drivers/Climate/Supplemental/Forests_and_Climate_Change.pdf

Coca Production, Deforestation and Climate Change
http://blogs.ei.columbia.edu/2010/03/24/coca-production-deforestation-and-climate-change/

Climate Change and the Amazon Rainforest - Amazon Watch
http://amazonwatch.org/work/climate-change-and-the-amazon-rainforest

Ecological restoration and global climate change
http://onlinelibrary.wiley.com/doi/10.1111/j.1526-100X.2006.00136.x/pdf

Rainforest burning and the global carbon budget: Biomass, combustion efficiency, and charcoal formation in the Brazilian Amazon
http://onlinelibrary.wiley.com/doi/10.1029/93JD01140/full

Land clearing and the biofuel carbon debt
http://www.sciencemag.org/content/319/5867/1235.short

Fossilized Tropical Forest Found — in Arctic Norway
http://www.livescience.com/52868-fossil-forests-norway.html
"During the Devonian period (416 million to 358 million years ago), Earth's first large trees were emerging. Also, around this time, atmospheric carbon dioxide dropped significantly. Scientists look to the earliest forests for evidence that tree growth played a part in scrubbing CO2 from the atmosphere — trees use the greenhouse gas to photosynthesize and form sugary food — contributing to the global cooling event that occurred at the end of the Devonian."

Half of all Amazonian tree species may be globally threatened
http://www.slate.com/blogs/future_tense/2015/11/18/global_temperatures_hit_new_high_amid_record_el_nino.html
"More than half of all tree species in the world's most diverse forest – the Amazon – may be globally threatened, according to a new study. But the study, published today in the journal Science Advances, also suggests that Amazonian parks, reserves and indigenous territories will protect most of the threatened species, if properly managed."
[16] You can find The Nature Conservancy on the web at http://nature.org/ and the Sierra Club at www.sierraclub.org/

World Wildlife Fund: http://www.worldwildlife.org/
Natural Resources Defense Council: http://www.nrdc.org/
Habitat For Humanity: http://www.habitat.org/
Commission for Environmental Cooperation: http://cec.org/
United Nations Environment Program: http://www.unep.org/
Water Partners International http://water.org
For a full list of Environmental Organizations:
http://en.wikipedia.org/wiki/List_of_environmental_organizations

Continental Divide Trail Coalition - https://continentaldividetrail.org/
Pacific Crest Trail Association https://www.pcta.org/
The Appalachian Trail Conservancy http://www.appalachiantrail.org
The International Appalachian Trail http://iat-sia.org/index.php
European Rambler's Association http://www.era-ewv-ferp.com/frontpage/
The Great Himalaya Trail http://trekthegreathimalayatrail.com/

For more organizations who could use your help, see Appendix C

[17] That is, without further reliance on man to provide chemical fertilizers, genetic strains immune to the toxicity of the fertilizer and nutrients necessary to feed those plants in a lifeless soil. But the effect is bland, tasteless and nutrition-less fruits and vegetables. The essence or spirit of the plant has been lost, replaced by an intellectual property owned and controlled by its patent holder.

See, *Extinction risk of soil biota*
http://www.nature.com/ncomms/2015/151123/ncomms9862/full/ncomms9862.html

*How soil is destroyed*
http://www.fao.org/docrep/T0389E/T0389E02.htm

*Soil Erosion and Degradation*
http://www.worldwildlife.org/threats/soil-erosion-and-degradation

Only 60 Years of Farming Left If Soil Degradation Continues
https://www.scientificamerican.com/article/only-60-years-of-farming-left-if-soil-degradation-continues/

Topsoil Erosion - Stanford University
http://large.stanford.edu/courses/2015/ph240/verso2/

*     *     *

Update: There are robust solutions out there based on mycelium. See:

*All Natural, Mushroom-Based Pesticide Could Revolutionize Agriculture*
http://reset.me/story/all-natural-mushroom-based-pesticide-could-revolutionize-agriculture/

*Mycelium Running: How Mushrooms Can Help Save the World* by Paul Stamets
http://www.amazon.com/Mycelium-Running-Mushrooms-Help-World/dp/1580085792/ref=sr_1_1?s=books&ie=UTF8&qid=1441575765&sr=1-1&keywords=Mycelium

[18] Which is nothing short of shocking that this should need to be explained to a food industry that no longer seems to recognize healthy soil as a pretty basic, self-evident requirement for any and all sustainable farming.

For more information on Biodynamic Farming, please visit:
https://www.biodynamics.com/

[19] Additional resources:
Uganda's Zika Forest, birthplace of the Zika virus
https://www.cnn.com/2016/02/02/health/zika-forest-viral-birthplace/index.html

Angiostrongyliasis (Rat Lungworm)
http://health.hawaii.gov/docd/disease_listing/rat-lungworm-angiostrongyliasis/

New cases of rat lungworm disease discovered on Hawaii Island
http://www.hawaiinewsnow.com/2019/03/29/new-cases-rat-lungworm-disease-discovered-hawaii-island/

Rat lung worm disease (Angiostrongylus cantonensis) factsheet
https://www.health.nsw.gov.au/Infectious/factsheets/Pages/rat-lung-worm.aspx

Chikungunya Virus
https://www.cdc.gov/chikungunya/index.html

Killer Zika-carrying mosquitoes are heading to the UK as global warming sees Britain get hotter and wetter, study predicts
https://www.dailymail.co.uk/health/article-6861713/Zika-dengue-threaten-billion-climate-warms.html

Scientist: Zika virus outbreaks that impacted pregnant women have almost disappeared
https://www.wsbtv.com/news/local/zika-virus-outbreaks-that-impacted-pregnant-women-have-almost-disappeared/934065385

A Billion People Will Be Newly Exposed to Diseases Like Dengue Fever as World Temperatures Rise
https://www.infectioncontroltoday.com/viral/billion-people-will-be-newly-exposed-diseases-dengue-fever-world-temperatures-rise

Mosquitoes that transmit the Zika virus and dengue fever may have access to 1 billion more people in the years ahead
https://www.businessinsider.com/mosquitos-carrying-zika-dengue-threaten-1-billion-more-people-2019-3

Skin-eating fungus is mighty species slayer
https://www.nature.com/articles/d41586-019-01002-2

The Worst Disease Ever Recorded
https://www.theatlantic.com/science/archive/2019/03/bd-frogs-apocalypse-disease/585862/?utm_source=feed

Deadly Fungus Has Decimated More Than 500 Amphibian Species » Focusing on Wildlife
https://focusingonwildlife.com/news/deadly-fungus-has-decimated-more-than-500-amphibian-species/

A Mysterious Infection, Spanning the Globe in a Climate of Secrecy
https://www.nytimes.com/2019/04/06/health/drug-resistant-candida-auris.html

[20] There are many good resources on the web. The UNESCO World Water Assessment page can be found here:

www.unesco.org/water/wwap/facts_figures/basic_needs.shtml

You can also find out more at The World Health Organization's Water, Sanitation and Health page:
 www.who.int/water_sanitation_health/en/

[21] Aquifers account for 97% of Earth's fresh water, in its liquid state. The largest source of fresh water in the world is in its frozen state, in Antarctica.

Aquifers Fact Sheet
https://www.safewater.org/fact-sheets-1/2017/1/21/aquifers

Environmental Technology and Preservation: The Pine Bush, Landfills, and Groundwater Integrity
http://ottohmuller.com/nysga2ge/Files/1995/NYSGA%201995%20B8%20-%20Environmental%20Technology%20And%20Preservation%20-%20The%20Pine%20Bush,%20Landfills,%20and%20Groundwater%20Integrity.pdf

Aquifer Variance Report… Application to Construct and Operate a Solid Waste Management Facility
http://www.capitalregionlandfill.com/documents/EIS_final/Appendix-I-Aquifer-Varinace-Report/Aquifer-Variance-Report-Final-Revision-4-7-09.pdf

[22] One risk of global climate change is that it could return us to a protracted and lengthy ice age. In actuality, we are in a period of interglaciation now.

> The current ice age, the Pliocene-Quaternary glaciation, started about 2.58 million years ago during the late Pliocene, when the spread of ice sheets in the Northern Hemisphere began. Since then, the world has seen cycles of glaciation with ice sheets advancing and retreating on 40,000- and 100,000-year time scales called glacial periods, glacials or glacial advances, and interglacial periods, interglacials or glacial retreats. The earth is currently in an interglacial, and the last glacial period ended about 10,000 years ago.
> https://en.wikipedia.org/wiki/Ice_age

The absurdity is that we have the technology now to solve all our energy needs through a variety of methods such as Liquid Fluoride Thorium Reactors and space-based solar power. Why even bother to debate the causes of global warming when we have the means to provide a long-term solution to all our global energy needs through LFTR or solar power? Obviously, there are other forces at work here.

> The dark ages still reign over all humanity, and the depth and persistence of this domination are only now becoming clear.
>
> R. Buckminster Fuller
> *Cosmography*, 01992

What we lack is political will. What we need is space-based solar power!

Space-based solar power (SBSP)
http://spaceenergy.com/SBSP/SBSP_Overview.htm

Space Energy | A Space Based Solar Power Company …
http://spaceenergy.com/home.htm

First the moon, now China plans to launch space-based solar power satellite
https://thehill.com/opinion/technology/431178-first-the-moon-now-china-plans-to-launch-space-based-solar-power-satellite

Why the Future of Solar Power Is from Space
https://singularityhub.com/2018/12/31/why-the-future-of-solar-power-is-from-space/#sm.000018rdzni6igea9u1uhm9zh0b55

> Dear reader, traditional human power structures and their reign of
> darkness are about to be rendered obsolete.

R. Buckminster Fuller
*Cosmography*, 01992

[23] *Bahala na.*<God willing.>

[24] SPF -- Synergetic Positive Feedback -- in action. See Appendix A for a brief trail description

[25] For example, the IPT follows the IAT – Morocco in Africa, the E4 - Gibraltar – Pyrenees – Lake Constance – Balaton – Rila – Kreta – Cyprus Trail in Europe, the Great Himalayan Trail through Kashmir, India, Nepal, Bhutan and Tibet, the Continental Divide Trail through North America, the TransPanama Trail in Central America and The Route of Parks in Chile.

IAT – Morocco – "The first phase of IAT Morocco will extend approximately 600 kms from Midelt to Taroudant."
http://www.iat-sia.org/index.php?mact=News,cntnt01,detail,0&cntnt01articleid=178&cntnt01returnid=15

E4 - Gibraltar – Pyrenees – Lake Constance – Balaton – Rila – Kreta – Cyprus Trail - at 10,450 km (6,493 mi,) this is considered the longest European trail. https://www.era-ewv-ferp.org/e-paths/e4/

Via Alpina – http://www.snipview.com/q/Via_Alpina

The Great Himalayan Trail – a 4,500-kilometer (2,800 mi) path stretching the length of the Greater Himalaya range http://greathimalayatrails.com/

Continental Divide Trail – "3000 miles through the Rocky Mountains from Canada to Mexico" http://www.cdtsociety.org/

Continental Divide of the Americas Trail
https://en.wikipedia.org/wiki/Continental_Divide_of_the_Americas#/media/File:NorthAmerica-WaterDivides.png

TransPanama Trail – "a long distance hiking route (approximately 700 mile-long) that traverses Panama from the border of Colombia to the border of Costa Rica, connecting a network of existing trails and rural roads." https://thetranspanamatrail.com/

The Route of Parks – "connecting 17 national parks stretching 1,700 miles from Puerto Montt in the north to Cape Horn in the south." http://www.rutadelosparques.org/
[26] "The delayed response is known as climate lag. The reason the planet takes several decades to respond to increased $CO_2$ is the thermal inertia of the oceans. Consider a saucepan of water placed on a gas stove. Although the flame has a temperature measured in hundreds of degrees C, the water takes a few minutes to reach boiling point. This simple analogy explains climate lag. The mass of the oceans is around 500 times that of the atmosphere. The time that it takes to warm up is measured in decades…"
https://www.skepticalscience.com/Climate-Change-The-40-Year-Delay-Between-Cause-and-Effect.html

"Climate lag is defined as a delay that can occur in a change of some aspect of climate due to the influence of a factor (s) that is slow-acting. An example of climate lag is the full effect of the release of a particular amount of carbon dioxide into the atmosphere…"
https://www.encyclopedia.com/environment/energy-government-and-defense-magazines/climate-lag

"The best estimate for the thermal lag delay is that it takes very roughly forty years* from the time we increase CO2 levels for most of warming to occur in response to that extra CO2…"
http://www.climatevictory.org/lags.html
[27] Global Reforestation efforts:
The Philippines Breaks World Record By Planting More Than 3 Million Trees In An Hour (02014)
http://thehigherlearning.com/2014/09/30/the-phillippines-breaks-wold-record-by-planting-more-than-3-million-trees-in-an-hour/

India Plants 50 Million Trees in One Day, Smashing World Record (02016)
https://news.nationalgeographic.com/2016/07/india-plants-50-million-trees-uttar-pradesh-reforestation/

India plants 66 million trees in 12 hours as part of record-breaking environmental campaign (02017)
https://www.independent.co.uk/news/world/asia/india-plant-66-million-trees-12-hours-environment-campaign-madhya-pradesh-global-warming-climate-a7820416.html

Three-North Shelter Forest Program (01978 – 02050): a 72-year project to plant the Great Green Wall, a 2,800-mile series of shelterbelts to restrict expansion of the Gobi Desert. https://news.nationalgeographic.com/2017/04/china-great-green-wall-gobi-tengger-desertification/

The Great Green Wall of the Sahara and the Sahel – on-going efforts to plant a drought-resistant forest roughly 9-miles wide and 4,750-miles long. https://www.greatgreenwall.org/about-great-green-wall
[28] Research: Planting Trillions of Trees Could Cancel Out CO2 Emissions https://futurism.com/planting-trillions-trees-cancel-co2-emissions?fbclid=IwAR2XV3DggPVseNThOhGJkhdISUIHYSZDeH8EmT3VR79XZJcHad4c5SaKmR4

China And India Have Contributed In Making The Planet Greener Than It Was 20 Years Ago http://www.thinkinghumanity.com/2019/03/china-and-india-have-contributed-in-making-the-planet-greener-than-it-was-20-years-ago.html

A natural solution to the climate disaster: Climate and ecological crises can be tackled by restoring forests and other valuable ecosystems, say scientists and activists https://www.theguardian.com/environment/2019/apr/03/a-natural-solution-to-the-climate-disaster

Sikhs aim to plant million trees as 'gift to the planet' https://www.theguardian.com/world/2019/apr/05/sikhs-sikhism-guru-nanak-550-anniversary-tree-planting

For Cash and Pride, Replanting Canada's Forests by the Millions https://news.nationalgeographic.com/2018/06/reforesting-canada-forests-youth-photography/

Restoring natural forests is the best way to remove atmospheric carbon https://www.nature.com/articles/d41586-019-01026-8

Other resources:
One Tree Planted
https://onetreeplanted.org

Plant a Billion Trees
https://www.plantabillion.org/

Organizing a Tree Planting Project
https://www.arborday.org/takeaction/volunteer/organize.cfm
[29] Additional resources regarding the melting permafrost, its effects on global climate and key indicators:

Methane and Frozen Ground
https://nsidc.org/cryosphere/frozenground/methane.html

What Is Permafrost? | NASA Climate Kids
https://climatekids.nasa.gov/permafrost/

What is permafrost?
https://ipa.arcticportal.org/publications/occasional-publications/what-is-permafrost

Here's What Scientists Know About the Risk of a Massive Global Methane Release
https://www.seeker.com/earth/climate/heres-what-scientists-know-about-the-risk-of-a-massive-global-methane-release

How Likely Is a Runaway Greenhouse Effect on Earth? The results of the latest analysis are not entirely reassuring…
https://www.technologyreview.com/s/426608/how-likely-is-a-runaway-greenhouse-effect-on-earth/

Thawing permafrost produces more methane than expected - Phys.org
https://phys.org/news/2018-03-permafrost-methane.html

Researchers Warn Arctic Has Entered 'Unprecedented State' That Threatens Global Climate Stability
https://www.commondreams.org/news/2019/04/08/researchers-warn-arctic-has-entered-unprecedented-state-threatens-global-climate

Key Indicators of Arctic Climate Change 1971 to 2017
https://iopscience.iop.org/article/10.1088/1748-9326/aafc1b/meta
https://www.youtube.com/watch?time_continue=3&v=asKIeN0pYTk

The Madness Driving Climate Catastrophe
https://www.truthdig.com/articles/the-madness-driving-climate-catastrophe/

Biodiversity across trophic levels drives multifunctionality in highly diverse forests
https://www.nature.com/articles/s41467-018-05421-z

[30] Sustainable development/farming, affordable housing, family planning, women's health, childhood and continuing education, psychological, spiritual, religious, social, financial, medical and legal services, etc. For example, Microcredits: https://grameenfoundation.org
[31] Forests and climate change Carbon and the greenhouse effect
http://www.fao.org/docrep/005/ac836e/AC836E03.htm

"Planting new forests, rehabilitating degraded forests and enriching existing forests contribute to mitigating climate change as these actions increase the rate and quantity of carbon sequestration in biomass."

Not just recycled sunlight: Biomass burning and its influence on global climate change https://www.iop.org/activity/groups/subject/env/prize/file_52569.pdf

Deforestation Facts - What is Deforestation? | NRDC
http://www.nrdc.org/energy/forestsnotfuel/

Forests and Climate Change – UNEP
http://www.unep.org/training/programmes/Instructor%20Version/Part_2/Activities/External_Drivers/Climate/Supplemental/Forests_and_Climate_Change.pdf

Coca Production, Deforestation and Climate Change
http://blogs.ei.columbia.edu/2010/03/24/coca-production-deforestation-and-climate-change/

Climate Change and the Amazon Rainforest - Amazon Watch
http://amazonwatch.org/work/climate-change-and-the-amazon-rainforest

Ecological restoration and global climate change
http://onlinelibrary.wiley.com/doi/10.1111/j.1526-100X.2006.00136.x/pdf

Rainforest burning and the global carbon budget: Biomass, combustion efficiency, and charcoal formation in the Brazilian Amazon
http://onlinelibrary.wiley.com/doi/10.1029/93JD01140/full

Land clearing and the biofuel carbon debt
http://www.sciencemag.org/content/319/5867/1235.short

Fossilized Tropical Forest Found — in Arctic Norway
http://www.livescience.com/52868-fossil-forests-norway.html
"During the Devonian period (416 million to 358 million years ago), Earth's first large trees were emerging. Also around this time, atmospheric carbon dioxide dropped significantly. Scientists look to the earliest forests for evidence that tree growth played a part in scrubbing CO2 from the atmosphere — trees use the greenhouse gas to photosynthesize and form sugary food — contributing to the global cooling event that occurred at the end of the Devonian."

Half of all Amazonian tree species may be globally threatened
http://www.slate.com/blogs/future_tense/2015/11/18/global_temperatures_hit_new_high_amid_record_el_nino.html
"More than half of all tree species in the world's most diverse forest – the Amazon – may be globally threatened, according to a new study. But the study, published today in the journal Science Advances, also suggests that Amazonian parks, reserves and indigenous territories will protect most of the threatened species, if properly managed."
[32] You can find The Nature Conservancy on the web at http://nature.org/ and the Sierra Club at www.sierraclub.org/  For more organizations who could use your help, see Appendix C
[33] World Wildlife Fund: http://www.worldwildlife.org/

Natural Resources Defense Council: http://www.nrdc.org/
Habitat For Humanity: http://www.habitat.org/
Commission for Environmental Cooperation: http://cec.org/
United Nations Environment Program: http://www.unep.org/
Water Partners International http://water.org
For a full list of Environmental Organizations:
http://en.wikipedia.org/wiki/List_of_environmental_organizations

The International Appalachian Trail http://iat-sia.org/index.php
European Rambler's Association http://www.era-ewv-ferp.com/frontpage/
The Great Himalaya Trail http://trekthegreathimalayatrail.com/

[34] That is, without further reliance on man to provide chemical fertilizers, genetic strains immune to the toxicity of the fertilizer and nutrients necessary to feed those plants in a lifeless soil. But the effect is bland, tasteless and nutrition-less fruits and vegetables. The essence or spirit of the plant has been lost, replaced by an intellectual property owned and controlled by its patent holder.

Extinction risk of soil biota
http://www.nature.com/ncomms/2015/151123/ncomms9862/full/ncomms9862.html

How soil is destroyed
http://www.fao.org/docrep/T0389E/T0389E02.htm

Soil Erosion and Degradation
http://www.worldwildlife.org/threats/soil-erosion-and-degradation

*     *     *

Update: There are robust solutions out there based on mycelium. See:

*All Natural, Mushroom-Based Pesticide Could Revolutionize Agriculture*
http://reset.me/story/all-natural-mushroom-based-pesticide-could-revolutionize-agriculture/

*Mycelium Running: How Mushrooms Can Help Save the World* by Paul Stamets
http://www.amazon.com/Mycelium-Running-Mushrooms-Help-World/dp/1580085792/ref=sr_1_1?s=books&ie=UTF8&qid=1441575765&sr=1-1&keywords=Mycelium

Update 2:
Pesticides Are Killing the World's Soils - They cause significant harm to earthworms, beetles, ground-nesting bees and thousands of other vital subterranean species
https://www.scientificamerican.com/article/pesticides-are-killing-the-worlds-soils/

[35] Which is nothing short of shocking that this should need to be explained to a food industry that no longer seems to recongnize healthy soil as a pretty basic, self-evident requirement for any and all sustainable farming.

[36] Please visit www.results.org for more information.

[37] There are many good resources on the web. The UNESCO World Water Assessment page can be found here: www.unesco.org/water/wwap/facts_figures/basic_needs.shtml you can also find out more at The World Health Organization's Water, Sanitation and Health page:
 www.who.int/water_sanitation_health/en/

[38] The risk of global climate change is that it could return us to a protracted and lengthy ice age. In actuality, we are in a period of interglaciaction now.

> The current ice age, the Pliocene-Quaternary glaciation, started about 2.58 million years ago during the late Pliocene, when the spread of ice sheets in the Northern Hemisphere began. Since then, the world has seen cycles of glaciation with ice sheets advancing and retreating on 40,000- and 100,000-year time scales called glacial periods, glacials or glacial advances, and interglacial periods, interglacials or glacial retreats. The earth is currently in an interglacial, and the last glacial period ended about 10,000 years ago.
> https://en.wikipedia.org/wiki/Ice_age

The absurdity is that we have the technology now to solve all our energy needs through space-based solar power. Why even bother to debate the causes of global warming when we have the means to provide a long-term solution to all our global energy needs through solar power? Obviously there are other forces at work here.

> The dark ages still reign over all humanity, and the depth and persistence of this domination are only now becoming clear.
> R. Buckminster Fuller, Cosmography

What we lack is political will. What we need is space-based solar power!

Space-based solar power (SBSP)
http://spaceenergy.com/SBSP/SBSP_Overview.htm

Space Energy | A Space Based Solar Power Company …
http://spaceenergy.com/home.htm

> Dear reader, traditional human power structures and their reign of darkness are about to be rendered obsolete.
> R. Buckminster Fuller, Cosmography

[39] *Bahala na.* <God willing.>

[40] SPF -- Synergetic Positive Feedback -- in action. See Appendix A for a brief trail description

[41] Sustainable Development, affordable housing, education, family planning, religious, social, financial, medical and legal services, etc.

About the Author

Düg Fresh is the author of several books including *The Children's Book of Colors: A journey from primary colors to the visual spectrum and how we see*, *A Thousand and One Appalachian Tales: A Journey along the A.T. and through the heart of Chapel Perilous* and *The Fictionary: A vocabulous flexicon of jocu-molecular jingo and colloquialiscious flapinations in the key of G*. He is also founder of the International Peace Trail Project, dedicated to the creation of "a footpath for those seeking fellowship with Earth" and to the idea that if you build it, peace will come. For more information on the IPT, please visit www.peacetrail.com He believes humor is the missing component to world peace and has developed a formula: $☮ = ♥ ☺^2$ ~ Peace equals love times happiness squared. See www.biggoof.org for more.

# Other books by Düg Fresh

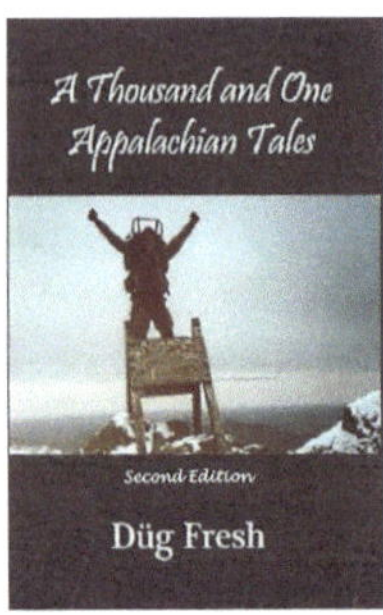

**A Thousand and One Appalachian Tales: A Journey along the A.T. and through the heart of Chapel Perilous – Second edition June 12, 02018   ISBN-13: 978-1983148484**

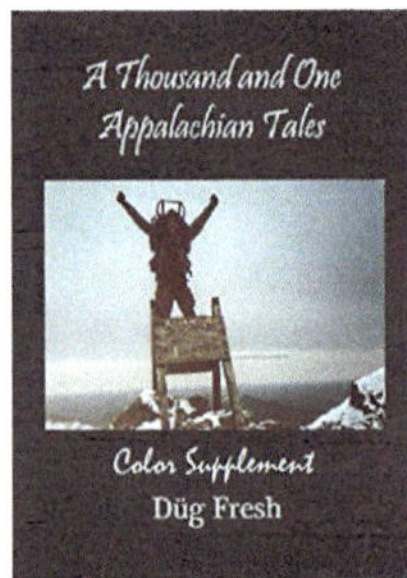

**A Thousand and One Appalachian Tales: Color Supplement – July 2, 02018 ISBN-13: 978-198332538**

**The Emperor's New Parade: A re-imagining of the Hans Christian Andersen classic for the darkest timeline – December 22, 02018  ISBN-13: 978-1792112621**

**The Fictionary: A vocabulous flexicon of jocu-molecular jingo and colloquialiscious flapinations in the key of G, 5th edition - August 30, 02019 ISBN-13: 979-8327513860**

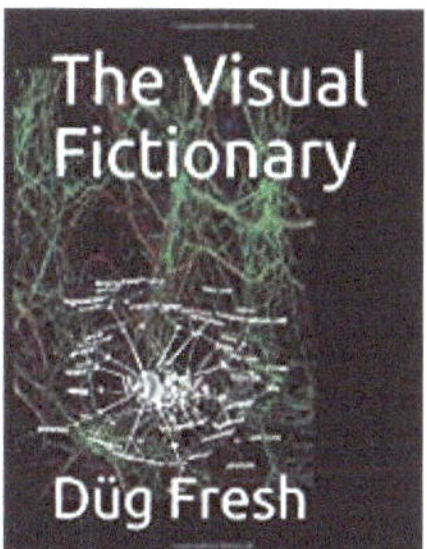

The Visual Fictionary: A vocabulous flexicon of jocu-molecular jingo and colloquialiscious flapinations in the key of G in color, visualized - Apr 10, 02018   ISBN-13: 978-1980527848

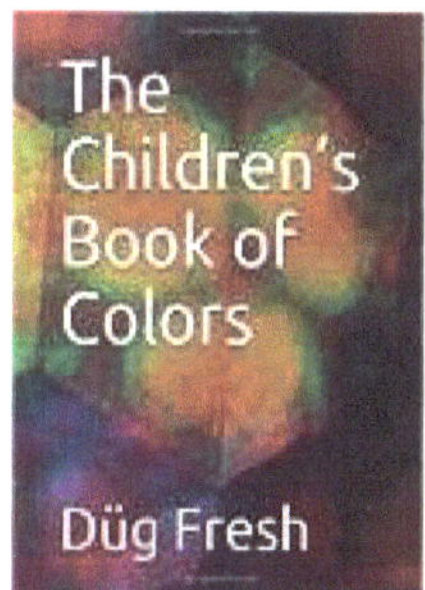

The Children's Book of Colors: A journey from primary colors to the visual spectrum and how we see – April 17, 02018   ISBN-13: 978-1980860655

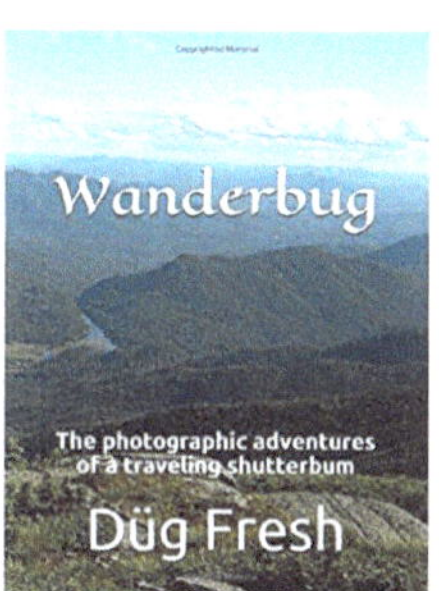

Wanderbug: The photographic adventures of a traveling shutterbum -  Volume One – February 11, 02020  ISBN-13: 979-8612519492

Fresh Digest Visualized: Computer-assisted exercises in a colorful ontology Paperback – January 13, 02023  ISBN-13 :  979-8373625593

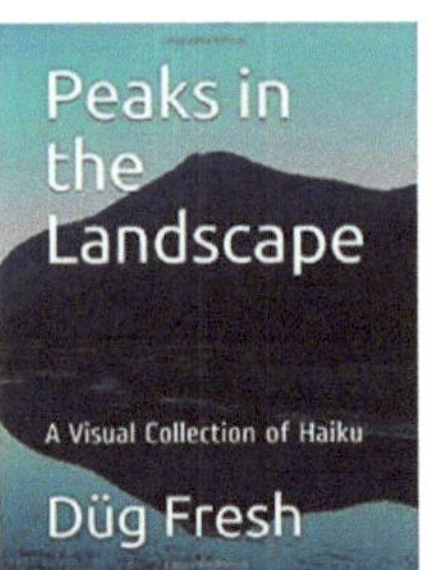

Peaks in the Landscape: A Visual Collection of Haiku – April 9, 02018   ISBN-13: 978-1980788256

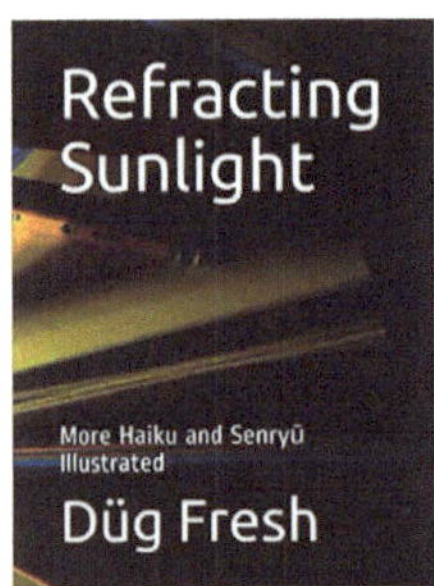

Refracting Sunlight: More Haiku and Senryū Illustrated – June 18, 02019  ISBN-13: 978-1074649838

Fresh Digest: The random thoughts of a photon navigating a labyrinth called the Multiverse – January 22, 02020  ISBN-13: 979-8602020250

Fresh Digest Volume Two: Further ramblings along the hallways of thought and madness from an infinite library in the Multiverse - November 23, 02020  ISBN-13 : 979-8569335589

Torres del Paine. Chilean terminus of the Internatonal Peace Trail

*A footpath for those seeking fellowship with Earth*

Peace, love and freshness be with you!